GRACE *at the* FINISH LINE

GRACE *at the* FINISH LINE

RECOLLECTIONS FROM A
NURSING HOME CAREGIVER

KATHY C. GUERRY

XULON PRESS

Xulon Press
2301 Lucien Way #415
Maitland, FL 32751
407.339.4217
www.xulonpress.com

Unless otherwise indicated, Scripture quotations taken
from the King James Version (KJV) – *public domain*.

Scripture quotations taken from The Message (MSG).
Copyright © 1993, 1994, 1995, 1996, 2000, 2001,
2002. Used by permission of NavPress Publishing
Group. Used by permission. All rights reserved.

Printed in the United States of America.

ISBN-13: 978-1-54564-188-0

1.

INTRODUCTION

I had worked in several different nursing specialties and found that each one has its own rewards and challenges. However, I was amazed at the intimate concern of nurses and personal care aides for their charges in long-term care or nursing homes. I had not witnessed in any other setting such fierce protection, knowledge, or insight into the needs of those committed to their care than with these nurses and aides.

From our residents' standpoint, I knew it had to be a daunting task to leave a home you have lived in for decades and cram everything you own into a 12 by 12-foot space, especially at a time when your mind, body, or both are struggling. For many of these folks, once they come through our doors, their vast world shrinks to these cubicle-sized rooms. For some, their admission was somewhat like dropping off the face of the earth. Very rarely a family member would take them out for supper or back home to participate in a special event. Many times, relatives and friends would never return to visit them.

Often we are asked how our staff can bear to work with such people in their debilitated states. After pondering why I enjoyed, and even loved, "these people," several things became clear. Family members held onto memories of their loved ones when they were younger, more physically and mentally fit. Those closest to them had witnessed many capabilities slip away and grieved each time one was lost. Now they looked through sadness and loss at what they considered a remnant of the loved one they knew. We, on the other hand, had no such memories of the people before, but simply accepted and celebrated each person just as he/ she was when the person came to us.

Like children, many of our charges have no filter and express freely what they think and feel. Just as young children had perhaps embarrassed their parents with this boldness, now the adult children are embarrassed when Mom or Dad have lost his/her tactfulness. They frequently apologize profusely when their parent is socially inappropriate. As for me, in a world of nuances, veiled references, and posturing, I happen to love it when an elderly resident just blurts out, "I don't like him," or "I'm not eating that!"

Very quickly, our clients become dependent on us. Day after day, they turn to us when they hurt, are lonely, or want to share a joke. That, my friend, is a sacred trust not to be taken lightly. We find ourselves coming to their aid, defending them, and going above and beyond what our duties demand. Many times a staff member will use his/her personal funds to obtain something "his/her" resident needs. A regular caregiver will be quick to take to task someone who fills in for him/her and doesn't meet his/her standard of care. Folks come in on their own time to style their ladies' hair just before a family visit or holiday. Believe me, they aren't thinking of a paycheck but of a person.

I experienced this recently with a client named Wilton Mack. Although I had never been assigned to care for him, I knew his history of mild mental retardation and end-stage renal disease. One Friday, he came to my desk and asked for a Snickers bar. He had few visitors and no relatives that I knew of, so there was nobody to leave candy or snack money for him. I took a trip to the vending machine, but the Snickers slot was glaringly empty. Mr. Mack sat silently waiting in front of my nurse's station. Someone called me to the phone around the same time, then I got busy and pretty much forgot him for fifteen minutes. Suddenly, I looked up from my desk and his eyes met mine. With a pang of guilt, I apologized, "Sorry; there are no Snickers bars in the building." I offered him a few other snacks. He said, "That's okay, never mind," and sadly rolled his wheelchair to his room.

I seldom left the facility for lunch, but that day I grabbed my sandwich and purse. Eating quickly in the car on my way to the store, I ran in and purchased a six-pack of Snickers bars. Mr. Mack was almost asleep when I placed the chocolate candy on his bedside table. His eyes flew open when he heard paper rattling. "Open it!" he said, grinning widely as he grabbed for one. I went back to my duties and never mentioned the candy to anyone.

Three days later, when I returned to work, I was shocked to find that Mr. Mack had suddenly taken ill and died the day before. Though saddened at this news, I was glad that I had listened to my heart the last time we were together. I can't tell you what motivated me to do what I did for him, but it's that sort of thing that makes me realize why we are there. It's difficult to describe the invisible bond that develops between nurses and patients. Often we can merely look at our charges and know that something is just not right with them. It's an honor to be allowed to walk beside them in the winter of their lives and to glean wisdom from their experiences.

A few years ago, I lived near a lake and enjoyed photographing the sunrises and sunsets. I would be hard-pressed to say which was more beautiful, but lately I tend to favor sunsets. Stunning sunrises are bright as they emerge expectantly from the night, full of promise for the unknown day ahead. In contrast, a golden sunset looks back knowingly at the brash sunrise. She has endured clouds and thunder, seen hail and ice; but she has survived and it is enough. Now having known accomplishment, she sighs with contentment and embraces the approaching night.

2.

IT ALL STARTED WHEN.....

I n the middle of a divorce, desperate to escape the quietness of my suddenly empty house on the weekends, I prayed for God to direct me to a second job. I felt Him leading me to a nearby nursing home; hardly a place for someone struggling through major life changes, downright depressing, many would say. However, after a few weeks, things began to fall into place. It amazed me how much I found in common with the residents I was assigned to care for regularly.

First there was William, who wanted to be touched or constantly engaged in conversation. One evening he requested I stop my charting and come walk with him. When I declined, gesturing to the stack of forms I needed to complete, he ordered, "Burn them." Like a young child placing his little hands on his mother's cheeks and turning her face toward his, he demanded eye contact. The moment you took your eyes off him, he ran away, activating the warning alarms as he exited the building. His mind might have been foggy, but there was nothing wrong with his legs. I was amazed at how fast he could completely disappear from sight. One very cold night, he slipped outside the building undetected. When the staff could not quickly locate him on the grounds, we had to call the police in with their helicopters and bloodhounds to finally find him.

Then I met Ms. Jerri, a retired nurse and mother. Though she has spent her life caring for others, now she had to rely on us to assist her with the simplest daily tasks. Her angelic face often furrowed in panic, as she expressed her constant fears aloud. "Who will help me?" she would ask. "Let me go with you. Please don't leave me. Who will take care of me? Oh, I'm so afraid!"

Next, I encountered Julie, a mildly retarded middle-aged lady with a cherubic face. Sweet as pie when she wanted to be, she could turn into a vicious, cursing tyrant when the notion struck her. Her family dropped her off at the door and never looked back.

She, unfortunately, had no visitors until her roommate's family came. Julie pounced on them immediately, declaring that her underwear had been stolen, all the while glaring at her roommate. The ensuing drama was so predictable and could only be resolved with intervention by the staff. When the nurses saw visitors entering the room, we flipped a coin to decide whose turn it was to fight the "great panty wars."

Was she testing the limits of her relationship with us? Was her hostility her way of asking if we will leave her once we see her for who she really was? Could it be that her come-close, go-away behavior was a protective mechanism to pre-serve what was left of her heart? The last time she loved somebody, things didn't end well for her. She could only watch as other residents received cards and letters. Christmas gifts never came from her family. If they deserted her, how could anyone else possibly care for her?

I had heard of the little man that shared his misery with the staff: Mr. Simon, known as the silently angry man. He was so angry that he's here or that he is alive, he will not speak. Oh, he had slipped up once or twice and uttered a few words so we know he is capable of speech. Disease has cost him his feet and legs, a piece at a time; the more the surgeons cut, the deeper he retreated into his dwindling self. His wounds had to be treated and dressed daily; although we talk to him during the process, he didn't speak. Was he hiding because he was afraid to expose any more of himself to this world where bad things were cut away? What if his words were unacceptable, will they cut out his tongue? Was it fear that made him hide his true self?

Last on my list is Smiling Susan. Susan was a young woman who beamed with love for her Savior. Her work as a loving wife and mother was cruelly interrupted by a crippling neuromuscular disease. As her aide bathed and fed her, I couldn't help but think that she should be bathing and feeding her children instead. How she must have longed to get up and care for them, for her mind was completely whole. Every word required great effort, yet she still sought to say thank you each time we tend to her. Her smile lit up the room and she never complained. She didn't care to watch TV, but her one request was that you keep the radio tuned to her favorite gospel station. I saw in Susan joy, patience, and thankfulness-virtues that we all could use more of in our lives.

The other residents' lives speak to me also. How many of us, like William, set off our own alarms because we have felt ignored or rejected? Don't we all have the same basic fears Ms. Jerri had, as we ask who will be there for me? Like sweet Julie, do we vacillate between expressions of extremes, needing someone's help, and at the same time being afraid to trust that our needs will be met? Perhaps Mr. Simon isn't the only one who retreats for fear of a world that he can't understand. While we bravely smile in public, are we really keeping silent about our pain, afraid of rejection if our true selves are exposed?

Looking back over these lessons, I'm amazed at the methods God uses to get the message across. He knew exactly where to send me. Thanks Susan for your example of gratitude and loving acceptance of a life that you have not chosen, yet still comes from the hand of a loving Father. Thanks for reminding me that life only makes sense when we stay tuned in to the things that matter most.

3.

SHE'S MY BROTHER

I couldn't help chuckling to myself as I heard Ms. Green approaching the day room. She shouted, "Good day, everyone," every time she came through a doorway. No matter what time it was, or whether she had just left us two minutes earlier, she always happily sang out her trademark salutation. When I learned that she had been employed as a greeter at Wal-Mart in her younger days, I nicknamed her "The Perpetual Greeter." She was ever so extremely polite and thanked anyone who rendered the least bit of assistance or attention to her. I watched as she wheeled her chair toward Ms. Morris's room. Ms. Morris's vocabulary consisted of one word, "Hey," but she would nod her head and use hand gestures. For some reason, today Ms. Green thought this lady was her brother. Ms. Morris did have an extremely short haircut and a slight figure. It would not be difficult to mistake her for a man.

"Good morning, Harold. I wanted to come see how you are doing. I heard you have been sick." Ms. Morris, who rarely had a visitor, happily shouted, "Hey!" Fearing one of the pair might become agitated when they discovered the mistaken identity, I decided to monitor the interaction from my position in the hallway, where I was hidden from their view.

Ms. Green continued, "Harold, I hope they are feeding you well. You know you need to eat to feel better." Ms. Morris was grunting. I imagined her hands waving, her head nodding in agreement. Ms. Green was so thrilled to see her "brother" that she failed to notice the feeding tube protruding from Ms. Morris's abdomen. A stroke had robbed her of the ability to swallow, and the dear lady had been unable to eat for the past five years.

"That's good," replied Ms. Green, "I'm so glad to hear that. I worry about you, you know. I'm so happy that you are feeling better. You are really looking good. How about Uncle Thomas and Aunt Sophie? Did they come by here and see you when they were here last week?" There was a brief pause and I assumed Ms. Green was happy with

"Harold's" reply, because she continued. "Harold, you know you are the only brother I have and I really care a lot about you. I feel so much better knowing that you are doing good." Ms. Morris answered, "Hey!" I was barely managing to control my laughter at the scene I imagined unfolding between the two ladies.

Ms. Green sang a chorus that she hoped her "brother" would remember from their childhood days in the church choir. Ms. Morris, who loved music, shouted "Hey, hey!" with enthusiasm at this point.

"Harold, you remember Momma's favorite scripture? Three John 1:4: 'I have no greater joy than to hear that my children walk in truth.'"

In a solemn, big-sister tone of voice, Ms. Green then reminded "Harold" to keep being a good boy and make their momma proud. Although I was not hearing any replies, she responded as though she was.

"O.K. Harold," Ms. Green began, "I have to go now but I love you and am so happy that I got to see you. Now that I know where you are, I will be coming back to check on you."

This was followed by Ms. Morris's animated "Hey!" I watched as Ms. Green came rolling out into the hallway. The phrase "and a good time was had by all" seemed a suitable description of their encounter. Ms. Morris was tickled pink with her mysterious visitor; and Ms. Green, having found her long-lost brother, was overjoyed.

"Good day, everyone!" Ms. Green shouted, as she wheeled past me and turned toward the exit. I caught up with her and bent down to speak into her ear.

"Ms. Green, it's time for lunch. May I take you over to your wing so you can eat?" Immediately she replied, "Thank you." As I began pushing her wheelchair, she shouted back at me, "You know I can't hear a single word you say, but I thank you anyway."

4.

A PERFECT
CHRISTMAS GIFT

The Christmas season always evokes images of trees, gifts and excited children. Carols, cards, creches, and candy canes fill our hearts and homes. Family functions are foremost in the minds of many, as tradition is never so evident as at this time of year. However, for those whose lives have been derailed by unexpected occurrences like illness, the death of a loved one, or the breakup of a marriage, Christmas can be a painful reminder. The traditions that we once found so comforting can now haunt us like Scrooge's shadows of Christmas past. Like the miserable Grinch, even the jolliest of us may feel our hearts shrinking and pinching. We don't have to slide down chimneys with empty bags and grimaces to find ourselves stealing the Yuletide joy from those around us.

When I encounter a Grinch or Scrooge (or am tempted to act like one myself), I remember an incident that epitomized the spirit of Christmas. Indeed, the attitude I witnessed is appropriate for every day of our lives.

I spent this particular Christmas Day on duty at the long-term care facility. During the holiday season, numerous churches and civic groups scheduled parties and brought small gifts. Many of our residents wouldn't receive holiday gifts or visits from their families. Without these enthusiastic volunteers, Christmas would be just another day for many of our them.

I shall never forget the group that came by to visit and distribute gifts that Christmas. I stood watching as the zealous cheer purveyors walked among the excited seniors. I watched as hands crippled by disease laboriously removed shiny bows, then opened brightly wrapped packages. Smiles of joy lit their faces, as they received bottles of lotion or boxes of candy.

Just a few feet away from me, an elderly gentleman sat in his wheelchair, patiently awaiting his turn. I could only hazard a guess at what he was thinking. Was he wondering what he would receive? Did he hope for chocolate-covered cherries or perhaps a bottle of aftershave? Was he remembering the gifts he had opened years ago, trinkets wrapped by his children when they were small? Perhaps the memory of a gift his wife had surprised him with the year before she died came to his mind. Possibly, he could be realizing that this may be the one and only package he will open this Christmas.

Finally, a smiling young man approached him with a small red box then stepped back in happy anticipation of the older gentleman's response. As the elderly man tore the gift-wrapping away and held up a pair of socks, I stifled a gasp of disbelief. Holding my breath now, I waited for his angry outburst. Had the young man failed to notice that the unfortunate man was a double amputee? How could he be so insensitive? Two scarred stumps were glaring quite obviously at this very moment. I half-expected him to throw the socks back at the thoughtless youth.

"Ah," my wheelchair-bound friend exclaimed, as he opened one sock and slipped it onto his hand, "This is just what I needed to keep these cold hands warm! Thank you very much, son."

The happy giver, validated by the old man's genuinely grateful smile, was already searching for his next recipient. Without a second glance, he hurried away; hurried right past the absence of shoes, socks, or feet in the chair before him. That gracious older man gave gratitude in exchange for socks, and he gave me a lesson I won't forget. It truly is more blessed to give than it is to receive, and perhaps even more so when we have what we feel is a less-than-perfect Christmas.

5.

CAN YOU SEE ME?

Have you ever wondered what a nurse might see in a typical shift? In my career, a day might include ripping off ingrown toenails, which is one of the goriest things I've had the displeasure of observing. Ranking in the top ten would be removing metallic fragments from someone's eye or watching a scalpel pierce tissue around a swollen, painful boil. Though not the same type of problem, it is truly painful to share the sorrow when a hopeful couple learns they will never be able to have the baby they dreamed of.

Someone may come in to receive the result of their recent biopsy, a nurse may see. Every malignant report has to be translated from its cold, sterile lab to the lives of flesh and blood people, some of whom the doctor and his staff have come to know and love. The dreaded prognosis, like a tiny pebble thrown into a peaceful pond, means their lives are forever changed.

I liken that impact of news to a fighter pilot dropping a bomb on an unsuspecting village. Like the pilot, untouched by his bomb, we may close the door when the patient leaves but this day is permanently etched into their memories, challenging their resolve and possibly their very existence.

Sadly, after repeated exposure, these things can become mundane.

They say it's hard to shock an old nurse because we have seen everything. Teenaged girls who got pregnant from toilet seats and swimming pools are commonplace; and don't even ask me about drug test results from "non-users." Then there is an entire category entitled "How Did That Get In There?" Bugs and beans climb into ears and noses. Bullet wounds appear in folks who swear they weren't shot. Women mysteriously get multiple broken bones with no recall of an injury. (Actually only those with abusive boyfriends or husbands suffer from this malady.)

I will spare you the really gross tales except for this one, which is quite possibly the worst thing I have ever seen. Things started out as just a normal day at the geriatric facility. There was really nothing unusual about the middle-aged man who showed up around lunch time, although none of the staff remembered seeing him visit before. He was clearly uncomfortable, as are many who step from the world of functioning minds and bodies to an environment of glaring disabilities. It was clear from this man's calloused, grease-stained hands that he worked hard for his money. The clean plaid shirt and blue jeans he wore were probably as dressed up as he got. The frayed hat he clutched anxiously had left a telltale ring around his balding head.

An aide who was working nearby greeted him and asked if she could help him find someone. "I'm looking for my mother, Mrs. Lewis," he replied. She escorted him to the table where his mother lay in her reclining wheelchair. Mrs. Lewis had just finished her baby food-consistency meal and resumed the singsong chant that she muttered day and night. It was obvious that this man who looked tough enough to wrestle a bull was fighting the urge to run away. Intimidated is too weak a word to describe his discomfort: fear, terror, anguish perhaps come closer.

As soon as her meal tray was removed, he shuffled over to stand in front of her. With his stubby fingers nervously twisting the brim of his cap, he bent down until he was a few inches from his mother's face. Pulling up a chair beside hers, he smiled tenuously.

"Hello Momma, it's me, Martin." The relentless babbling didn't change pitch as she stared blankly ahead. "I-I'm your son, Momma. Don't you know me? Look at me, Momma, it's Martin."

Lord, I prayed, let her show some tiny response to him, something, anything at all. The room fell silent as his despair seemed to envelop the onlookers. It seemed that everyone held their breath at the same time, willing his mother to recognize him. Totally oblivious to his surroundings, the strong man pleaded pitifully, like a small child, for his mother's affirmation. She offered nothing, not a move of her hand toward him nor a shift of her eyes. The chanting continued without missing a beat. The tension in the room was palpable. From my position at the nurse's desk, I felt we were intruding on a very private, painful moment.

Soon it became evident that the poor fellow was getting nowhere. It seemed the thin veneer of self-control was crumbling before our eyes. Steeling my own emotions, I walked over to introduce myself to Martin. Explaining that I was Mrs.

Lewis's nurse, I advised, "We think her vision is really poor these days and the doctor suspects she doesn't hear very well now."

In reality, it was quite possible that the man before her didn't even exist in her mind. She may remember him as a sandy-haired lad playing around her feet. Or perhaps she had regressed to her own childhood and had no recollection of being a wife or a mother. There is so much that experts don't understand about this cruel disease. How could I expect this unsophisticated man to comprehend it? All he cared at this moment was that his mother did not know him. He was as desperate as a beggar starving for a crumb, but the one who gave him life had nothing to offer.

I wish I could tell you that she turned, gazed lovingly at him, and smiled. I wish I could say that Martin left there feeling much better than when he came. The truth is, there was no moment of recognition, no sudden lighting up of Momma's eyes. She remained trapped in her own world, where the door was closed and barred.

With an agonizing look on his face, Martin finally stood to his feet. I knew we would never see him again. Forcing a smile, I touched his arm lightly. "I'm sorry she can't communicate with you," I said. "Thank you for visiting her. At some level of consciousness, your voice is familiar to her and she has to be comforted by your presence here. Please know that we take care of her every need and she is not in pain." At least not physical pain, I think to myself. "We will let you know if there is any change in her condition."

I tried to sound professional and cheerful, but I couldn't help picturing my own son in Martin's shoes. With a sigh, he backed away from her. As he donned his hat, he thanked us for caring for his mom. "She was a really pretty lady and a wonderful mother," he noted sadly.

After he left, I wheeled his mom to her room. There on her nightstand was a picture of a beautiful lady, someone I imagined would be confident and directing preparations for a grand social gathering. She wore a gorgeous deep blue dress with a glistening strand of pearls. Her makeup was perfect; her face lit up in a smile that reached her eyes. The photo didn't look staged at all, but one felt the photographer had been merely passing by and accidentally caught her as she was busily enjoying life.

In one last attempt to connect the lady in the picture with the person who laid helpless before me, I bent down close to her ear and patted her arm. "Mrs. Lewis, that boy you raised, Martin, has grown into a good man and I know you are so proud of him. Good job, Mother." The chanting persisted as she gazed upward at nothing.

6.

VIVACIOUS VICTORIA

I shall never forget this gentle Southern lady with features as delicate as a china doll. Her daughter had been the caregiver but was now faced with illness herself and very reluctantly brought Victoria to us. Victoria enjoyed excellent physical health and walked as fast as she could around our facility. Like a motorized toy that had been wound too tightly, it seemed that she could not keep still for more than a few moments.

Victoria was blessed to have a very loving family, who visited her nearly every day. They were extremely attentive and could read her non-verbal cues. Her guests enjoyed pampering her with the loveliest clothing, hairstyles, and mani-cured nails. Victoria seemed accustomed to such royal treatment and accepted it graciously.

Her speech was largely incomprehensible by the time she came to us. Before dementia claimed her faculties, she had served as pianist for her church. When a friend visited and allowed Victoria to sit on the piano stool as she played, Victoria suddenly placed her fingers on the keys and played. When the old hymns were sung, although she could not tell you her own name, the dear lady would often sing every word flawlessly.

Victoria wouldn't sit in a wheelchair but because her gait was unstable, she required a special type of walker called a combo walker. This marvelous invention with protective bars, wheels, and a comfort seat allowed her to walk safely and independently.

Unfortunately, dementia caused some of Victoria's inhibitions to decrease and, much to the consternation of her peers, she could not keep her hands to herself. Always affectionate, she attempted to hold any hand she could find. Though I am certain that she meant no harm to anyone and would never have caused discomfort purposely, her fellow residents misinterpreted her friendly advances and avoided her. This, of course, upset amiable Victoria, who would then retreat to a corner to cry and tremble.

It was difficult to monitor her whereabouts because she moved so quickly. Even so, it seemed I spent a large part of my day running interference, as I could not bear to see this tender soul traumatized.

About this time, a series of changes in my personal life had sent me into a time of introspection. Approaching my sixtieth birthday, I reflected on turns my life had taken. One of my friends had recently entered the ministry and the church she pastored was doing very well. My son-in-law had moved our daughter and their children to South America on an extended missionary assignment. Even my younger sister had accepted a ministerial position. These things led me to question, as John the Baptist had after he was imprisoned, whether I had missed my calling to impact my world. How could I be effective in this obscure setting, with people that few even knew existed? Was anything I was doing really making a difference at all?

My answer came in a mysterious way and involved Ms. Victoria. It came in a dream so vivid that even now I have difficulty speaking of it. In this dream, I saw that Victoria was sitting in her walker in dismay, as her amicable overtures had once again been rejected. She had stopped in the middle of a busy hallway and would surely be jostled about as other residents in wheelchairs approached. Typically, we don't pull wheelchairs but push them from behind to prevent the occupant from becoming disoriented. In my dream, I quickly took hold of the front of her walker and pulled her away from the oncoming traffic. When I looked back to see her face, Victoria was no longer in the chair. The face I saw was brilliantly aglow, and I knew I was looking into the face of God.

Instantly, a memory flashed into my mind. "The King will say, I'm telling you the solemn truth: Whenever you did one of these things to someone overlooked or ignored, that was me—you did it to me" (Matt. 25:40). In the background, I heard, "Rescue the perishing, care for the dying," a song that I barely knew.

Overwhelmed by what I had seen and heard, I woke up weeping. I had been reminded that God was very much concerned about every detail in the lives of "the least of these." Just that quickly, my questions and doubts were instantly dissolved.

7.

THE MAN IN ROOM 108

O h for heaven's sake, there it goes again. At the absolute busiest time of the day, Mr. Alders just had to call for help. Although everyone knew he didn't actually need anything, he was persistent and his requests were as regular as clockwork. Honestly, I would have been more sympathetic if he did need something that our staff could have provided him. The morning shift was ending and the crew was scurrying around to complete their last-minute tasks before clocking out for the day. At the same time, the afternoon caregivers were reporting for duty and requesting updates on their patients. For the first few minutes, it was loud and could get hectic, especially if someone was tardy or new to the routine. The patients who were capable of understanding usually tried not to interrupt this brief baton-passing period. Everyone that is, except for Mr. Alders, the man in room 108.

I did feel sorry for him, for indeed Mr. Alders could do nothing for himself. Formerly an independent, very physically fit gentlemen, he had suffered strokes that rendered his arms and legs nearly useless. His surly attitude evidenced his discontent at the indignities of being totally helpless. Nevertheless, our staff members were very professional and usually managed to maintain cheerful attitudes as his daily cares were carried out.

On those days when my work flow was smooth and manageable, I found I didn't mind Mr. Alders' inopportune summons so much. However today, when I was struggling just to keep my head above water, I found myself sighing heavily. Glancing at his call light, for the first time a question occurred to me. Why does this happen at this exact time every day? This has to be more than coincidence. Why this pattern?

"Hello there, Mr. Alders," I literally sang as I entered his room, "Is there something I can do for you?" He looked pitifully small in the bed that seemed to engulf his shriveled limbs. His cookies and milk were placed strategically on the overbed table that was positioned perfectly over his torso.

His face displayed its usual scowl. "I just want to know who is taking care of me this afternoon," he demanded. Breathing a prayer for patience, I pointed to the orientation board hanging on the wall directly in front of his bed. "Hmm, it says here that Esther is your aide for second shift. How's that sound?" He knew as well as I did who his caregiver would be so why was he asking? There must be something he wasn't saying. "Is there anything else I can help you with today?" I asked kindly. Then I went slowly through my nurse's list: "Are you having any pain, would you like to get up, can I call someone for you?" He shook his head after each question. "I just wanted to know who's coming at three, that's all," he insisted. "Oh, I'm so glad I could help you. Please call if you need anything else. I will see you at supper, if not before."

I surveyed his room one last time, as if I'd never seen it before. I tried to put myself in his shoes. How must he feel in here? Perhaps powerless; completely incapacitated. He was unable to come to the desk and ask for anything. Someone first had to assist him into his wheelchair. He couldn't hold his own spoon at mealtime, couldn't get the urinal when he needed it. How awful it must be to depend totally on others for every little move you make. The only thing he could do was press his call light and ask for help. I looked again at his bed, positioned by the window. There was really nothing to see outside but trees and a distant view of the visitor's parking lot. If his roommate's curtain was pulled, Mr. Alders couldn't see if someone walked down the hall. I'm certain that he felt isolated, vulnerable.

I wondered if perhaps Mr. Alders feared being abandoned. Carol, the morning shift aide, knew where he was, and he was never anxious as long as she was on duty. Could it be that he feared her successor would forget about him or perhaps not know she was supposed to take care of him?

I tested my hypothesis the following day. Mr. Alders seemed satisfied all morning and offered no complaint. Carol had a special rapport with him. Nothing made him really happy but his irritability was dialed down to a much lower level when she was caring for him. She always came in on time and followed the same routine daily. Afternoon shift, by contrast, was quite inconsistent. Seldom would he have the same person tending him two days in a row. It was clear now that his anxiety level soared as Carol bid him good-bye. His call light rang incessantly for the first half-hour.

The nurses and staff began teaming up to decrease his nervousness by checking on him more frequently during this time of transition. Indeed, we could see positive results after a few days of reassuring Mr. Alders that although his caregiver changed, his level of care would remain constant. He wasn't as worried or demanding as he had been previously.

Unfortunately, he did not express appreciation for our efforts nor did his personality improve. If we ever forgot to extend that little extra at shift change, he reverted back to lighting up the nurse's desk.

Nancy, his nurse for the day, walked into his room one evening and was shocked to find Mr. Alders had died quietly in his sleep. It fell my lot to notify his family, then call the undertaker to remove his body.

After escorting the undertaker to Room 108, Nancy and I returned to the desk. Suddenly a call bell rang out. We were a bit surprised, as it was late and most of our residents were asleep. The light that came on was from Room 108, but that couldn't be; only Mr. Alders was in that room. We looked at each other and suddenly I laughed. "I forgot to tell Mr. Alders who is going to be taking care of him, now that the next shift has begun. You know he always gets nervous when somebody new comes on duty!"

The undertaker came out into the hallway with a puzzled look. "I promise I didn't touch that call light; I don't know why it came on," he said. Shaking his head, he returned to the room and re-emerged a few minutes later, pushing the gurney down the quiet hallway. Nancy and I just smiled. The call light never lit up on its own again after that night.

8.

FANCY
MEETING YOU HERE

I n spite of the usual challenges that accompanied
an admission, I found myself looking forward
to each one. None of us actually enjoyed the reams
of forms that must be filled out, the preparation
of room and roommate, procurement of medical
supplies for the new resident, and the introduction of our staff to the anxious family. Not to men-
tion there was the daily flow of routine duties that
must be completed simultaneously.

For me, the tedious administrative process was
eclipsed by an excitement akin to finding a new
book. Each person was a mysterious story that I
had not yet read. I was always amazed at the history that accompanied the often frail and elderly
figure — this person I would now be taking care of.
The information given by family and physicians

was our first introduction, but we had learned to take all that with the proverbial grain of salt.

Indeed, there was nothing in our newest resident's medical records to prepare us for her gruff demeanor. We would have to experience that firsthand.

Watching as Ms. Gertie came through the door, I thought, *Uh-Oh, this could be challenging*. I could tell by the fire in her eyes and the stern set of her jaw that this lady was as tough as nails. I surmised that her life had been hard. A lesser woman may have capitulated and quit, but this sassy lady hadn't lost her spunk.

Ms. Gertie looked to be about eighty-five, and I had no doubt she could fill a book with tales that would shock us. "The boys," her sons and grandsons, were right respectful of her, as they related witnessing her fistfights with men and women through the years. Unfortunately for her, she was now confined to a wheelchair. This may have given us an advantage. Perhaps we could at least run a little faster than she could wheel if she got after us.

I was relieved to hear that Ms. Gertie had softened some in her later years and had even become a regular Sunday School scholar. Her language was still quite colorful, and she often laughed about her exploits in the days of her rambling and carousing. She wanted to be sure we knew that an accident had caused her disability. She never lost a fight, she told us, with a look that implied she didn't intend to lose any either.

Ms. Gertie was unaware, as were we, that an old friend of hers resided four doors down the hall from her. It just so happened that Grace had grown up in the isolated rural area with Ms. Gertie, back in the days before electricity and indoor plumbing. Folks pretty much ate what they grew, caught, or shot. In their early years, most only had a mule and wagon for transportation.

Grace had noticed the flurry of activity that announces the arrival of a new resident. Curiosity drew her toward the nurse's desk. The two crusty divas met in the hall and loudly caught up on the past twenty years. They laughed about the fights they used to get into together, then switched to discussing their preachers and the goodness of the Lord.

Ms. Gertie's family was thrilled to see that her adjustment would be much smoother than they had anticipated due to Grace's presence. Oh, she lit the place up for a while. With her deep, gravelly voice, many of our residents found her intimidating. Ms. Gertie had no tolerance for whining, and she enjoyed taunting other residents who continually complained. When she wanted something, she would yell curse words and threats. Luckily for us, the three nurses she aimed her fists at happened to be the fastest gals on our unit. In another stroke of good luck, we found and confiscated the knife under her pillow before she tried to use it. Overall though, her transition went pretty well. We soon found the way to her heart with coffee and sweet snacks. I am not above bribing folks with food when the situation warrants it.

We all grew to love Ms. Gertie, who made sure we were never bored. After hearing some of the hardships she had faced, we came to admire her strength and humor. It was evident that her rough outer shell belied a marshmallow heart. She became the favorite of quite a few staff members. If we ever missed Grace or Ms. Gertie, we knew we would find them sitting together, chatting as if they'd never been apart.

Unfortunately, Ms. Gertie's health began to fail after she had been with us for about six months. She soon lost the ability to get in and out of her bed or chair without assistance. Having been such a strong, independent sort, this really caused her grief. Now, instead of standing guard between her and other residents, we were very careful to preserve her dignity. Grace visited her often, encouraging her to eat and to stay as physically active as possible.

All too soon the time came when the nurses noticed that Ms. Gertie was rapidly declining. The family visited more often, realizing it was only a matter of time. We figured she had at least a month left. The next week was rough for her, but she bounced back and seemed to regain some strength.

Monday morning came and she was the first person on my visiting list. The night nurse was happy to report that Ms. Gertie had slept well.

Cheerily, I called out to her as I entered her room. Usually the first thing she asked for was her hairbrush, makeup, and then coffee. I was alarmed when she didn't answer. However, she stirred a little when I touched her arm. Quickly checking her vital signs, I realized that her condition was critical. After calling the desk to notify the doctor and her family, I raised the head of her bed and assured her that we would stay with her. I realized it would be several hours before her family arrived, and I feared Ms. Gertie didn't have that much time left. With barely a second thought, I rushed to Grace's room. There was a chance that Grace would be adversely affected by watching her friend die. However, I really felt Ms. Gertie needed a friend or family member beside her. Kneeling beside Grace's wheelchair, I told her that Ms. Gertie wasn't going to make it and I asked if she would like to sit with her during her last hours. Grace replied, "Oh, yes, please take me to her."

Her friend of sixty years was fading fast but Grace was a champ, holding Ms. Gertie's hand, talking, and praying with her until she drew her last breath.

Checking my watch to note the time of her death, I was surprised to see that barely twenty minutes had passed since Grace and I had sat beside her.

"I'm so sorry, Grace, I thought she had more time. She was doing so much better when I last saw her on Friday. I didn't want to upset you, but I really felt she needed you here."

Drying her tears, Grace replied that she was thankful she'd been allowed to sit with her dear friend. By the time the family came in, Grace was composed and began to comfort the family. Together they remained in Ms. Gertie's room for several hours, sharing tears and laughter as they rehearsed memories of their experiences with this remarkable woman.

I was amazed at God's grace in bringing these ladies together again. In the safety and comfort of their friendship, they came to terms with the joys and sorrows of their lives. There were several facilities available to both families in our area. Our facility had a hundred beds to choose from. What was the possibility that these two would find themselves in the same facility and just a few doors apart at this critical juncture of their lives?

Our admissions coordinator generally assigns resident's rooms, but I suspect Someone a bit higher up already had this assignment well in hand.

9.

KISSES FOR COOKIES

With a ready smile and failure to feel sorry for himself, Sammy was one of my favorite residents. A brilliant biologist and a proud military veteran before the dementia robbed him, he was ever the gentleman. Sammy had lived and worked most of his life in the northeastern part of the United States. He had been widowed after his children were grown and later remarried. A dozen years later, he ended up at our nursing facility.

Sammy was in great physical condition and was the fastest walker we had seen in quite a while. Articulate and polished, he could easily convince visitors to help him escape the building. He was able to outline in detail his plan to hail a taxi, get to the airport, and report to work. His sympathizers were often shocked to learn that he was a resident and his job had ended twenty years ago. The staff could reason with Sammy, but his comprehension was fleeting. His mind could not retain the explanation for more than ten minutes, and then it was necessary to start again at square one. If he ever succeeded in getting through the door, several staff members would be in hot pursuit. Often Sammy had to be coaxed back into the building with a snack or a promise to call a taxi. He was so pleasant and agreeable that we caught ourselves laughing at his antics.

Once Sammy overheard several nurses converting a measurement from metric to standard. Unexpectedly, he stated that he knew the answer, then gave us the formula to calculate it. To our great delight, he was exactly right. From then on when a math question arose, someone would respond, "Just ask Sammy."

Unfortunately, Sammy had a bad fall and ended up with a shattered knee. There was nothing that could be done to restore function and he was never able to stand alone again. Forgetting that he now could not balance, he would try to rise and topple forward. After a few of these episodes, he was fitted with a special low-angle chair. From a semi-reclining position, he could wheel the chair about while the lowered hip angle prevented him from standing.

As his disease progressed, Sammy lost the ability to speak, but he was ever cheerful and liked to keep up with everything that went on in the building. Often he would make his rounds and was quick to note the addition of a new resident's name on the door. Without fail, he was the first one to roll over to the newcomer and extend his hand in welcome.

With the exception of maintenance and dietary, our staff was all female. Sammy quickly took on the role of protector and somehow always showed up at the desk anytime an unfamiliar male appeared. He was accustomed to seeing me behind the desk, amidst stacks of paperwork. Once a nurse who was unknown to him came over to borrow supplies while I was away from the desk. Sammy began yelling and pointing at her. He couldn't get the words out, but he knew she was not supposed to be behind my desk.

As Sammy's condition deteriorated, he resorted to gesturing to the staff when he wanted something. Any time he was addressed, he would reply with unintelligible "words" and a big smile. Often I entertained wishful thoughts of the movie

"Awakenings," where Robin Williams played a doctor who was able to temporarily restore the minds of his clients; but that was not to be for Sammy. We did become pretty proficient at deciphering his charades and established a fairly successful language of sorts.

Sammy's wife was faithful to visit him frequently. One day when she came, she found him on the other side of the facility. I passed them as she was pushing him down the hall, all the while chastising him for roaming the building. As I passed by, he caught my eye, pointed back at his wife, and, with a big smile, rolled his eyes in her direction. I could literally imagine him saying, "She's at it again!" In reality, he would never openly defy her and always greeted her with a kiss. He may not be able to walk or talk, but he knew he needed to keep "wifey" happy.

Sammy loved cookies and milk but not everyone understood his requests now. One day, he began motioning and I could tell he was getting a little frustrated. Many times, I'd seen residents get quite angry when they couldn't make themselves understood, but Sammy was still courteous. A few minutes later, when I returned with cookies and milk, he beckoned me to come closer.

As I leaned forward, expecting some sort of whispered appreciation, Sammy surprised me with a kiss on my cheek. The sweetness of his gesture nearly brought me to tears. Soon his snack break was over and Sammy happily returned to his post as security guard.

He was the first one I looked for when arriving in the morning, and the look on his face would usually be a barometer of the mood on the unit. If there was a new resident causing a disturbance, Sammy would gaze solemnly in that direction. If things were calm and orderly, Sammy would indicate that with a nod.

It's amazing how many good-natured residents became downright mean when they developed dementia. Changes in behavior and personality are often more troubling to family members than the physical effects of this cruel disease. Although Sammy's mental faculties declined little by little, miraculously he retained his gentlemanly ways until the very end. As for me, every time I see milk and cookies, I smile at the memory of Gentleman Sammy's grateful kiss.

10.

FIRST LOVE

Carefully he backed the family car out of his driveway and started the journey to her home. His chores for the day were finished and his appetite for food was gone. If he was quick about it, he could be with her in maybe ten minutes. His folks weren't very happy about that prospect. Just last night they tried to convince him to wait until the weekend to see his angel, but he thought of her constantly. Though he understood why the family pleaded with him to slow his pursuit of her, he couldn't help himself. Maybe if he was back before night falls, they won't even know he'd been gone. He must use extreme caution because they continued to inspect the car frequently for any damage. Who cares that they don't trust his driving? With great effort, he forced himself to drive slowly. He was almost there; it won't be long. Patience, patience, he told himself. He simply couldn't afford an accident or his keys would be confiscated.

Finally, her home came into view. With a pounding heart and sweaty hands, he whispered a prayer of thanksgiving. Will she be as happy to see him this time? Will that marvelous smile reassure him that he is still the one her heart has chosen? He was thrilled to be with her, even though all he could do for now was hold her hand, maybe kiss her on the cheek. The lovers had to be so careful because of their age. They both realize they couldn't be alone together, but they waited patiently, knowing that they would soon be forever inseparable; and time won't matter. They knew the love they had for each other was once in a lifetime and was worth waiting for.

This Romeo and his love were not teenagers but husband and wife, wed sixty years ago. Now because of dementia, she could no longer feed or dress herself. Residing in a geriatric facility near the house they raised their children in, her words would no longer come. Almost imperceptibly, she was losing bits of the person she was. Her silver hair framed a face lined with scars of time. A stunning smile, reserved only for him, spread across her lips when he walked in. He was just in time to feed her supper. Then holding her hand, he spoke to her in a way that only lovers understood.

If our staff had to enter the room while he was there, we walked on tiptoes and spoke in muffled tones. The very atmosphere in the room seemed charged with an electricity, a depth of emotions that were nearly tangible. It was almost like walking into the middle of a church service.

She had forgotten many things, including her children; but for now, she remembers him. Nobody knows what tomorrow holds but all is well today.

Perhaps the thrilling stories we see in the movies aren't the most accurate depictions of love. I suspect that genuine devotion isn't to be found in his bank account or even in her flawless physical beauty. Conversely, real love is unconcerned with transient attractions and endures the test of time.

He knows that one day, she may not remember who he is anymore. but he will remember her and that will be enough.

11.

WHAT'S THAT NOISE?

There have been numerous lighthearted moments along the way. As I was making rounds on my unit at the nursing home recently, I heard an eighty-eight-year-old lady calling out for help. Stepping into her room, I saw that her legs were hanging over the side of her bed. It only took a moment to reposition her and straighten the covers on her bed. We chatted for a moment and as I prepared to leave, I asked if she needed anything else. She replied that her throat bothered her. Surprised, I responded, "Does your throat hurt?" Immediately I began thinking of sore throat cures and causes. With a look of dismay, she quickly replied, "Oh no, it doesn't hurt. It's just that when I talk, it makes me sound like an old woman."

Then there was an obstinate elderly man who was known to be oppositional. One day he suffered a fainting episode. Sally, Dell, and I rushed to his room to revive him. After a few moments, his eyes fluttered slightly but he would not respond to our questioning. Sally gently shook his arm and shouted, "Mr. Gregg, Mr. Gregg, can you hear me?" Without moving or opening his eyes, Mr. Gregg responded clearly, "No!"

12.

CONCLUSION

Having head knowledge that God's grace is sufficient for our every need is quite different somehow from having experiential knowledge of that same concept. That reminds me of a story I heard about a little boy who was afraid to sleep alone. In the night, he cried out for his mother. She reassured him that he was not alone, as the angels were watching over him. He was quiet for a short time and then cried out again that he was afraid. His mother repeated the promise of unseen comforters in his room. The young lad responded, "I know there are angels, Mom, but right now I need somebody with skin on." I found some amazing people who fleshed out God's promise of grace in many different ways.

Being a newbie to geriatric care, I was blessed to have many exceptional coworkers. The nursing staff and supervisors were, for the most part, compassionate and competent in their nursing skills. They were always willing to share their experience and knowledge with newcomers. Many times I was moved to tears as I observed the genuine love and kindness exhibited by staff members who went above and beyond the scope of their duties. Nursing assistants were seldom celebrated, but I have encountered some who considered their work a high and holy calling. Even though they were on the low end of the pay scale, they took every routine task seriously and treated their charges with dignity.

One of the janitors, Jules, seemed to have an uncanny radar. He always had a funny anecdote, a firm handshake, or just a few moments to sit and listen to a resident who was ill, lonely, or depressed. Without fail, he exhibited the utmost respect and concern for each resident, no matter their physical condition.

I have been humbled and, at the same time, challenged by these emissaries of grace. It has been my goal to maintain the same high standard of care. My hat is off to the multitude of unsung heroes who are making a difference in the lives of those entrusted to their care.

CPSIA information can be obtained
at www.ICGtesting.com
Printed in the USA
LVHW04s1918270818
588257LV00001B/2/P